The Hue and The Ghost

Gustavo Lapis Ahumada

Copyright 1998

Dedicated to all the Warriors of the Heart.

True Love is Worth every Tear.

These Eyes	6
If I had your Kiss	7
Walls	9
Downward Spirals	11
Creole Charm	14
Palero's Night	15
A Breath Away	19
At the Foot of my Bed	20
When the Stars Give Way	22
Stand	23
King	24
Every Dream Shattered	27
Dare my Heart Ponder?	28
Show Me This	29
That In-between Place	30
Noise	31
Roar	33
Words	34
If the Sea were to Sway	36
Brittle Sea of Misplaced Souls	37
Beauty and Strength	39
My Beloved	40
Indigo Girl	42
The Hue and The Ghost	44
The Good Rain	47
Fireflies	49
November Dawn	50
We Glide over Stars	51
A Prayer of Gratitude	52
About the Author	53
Useful Links …	55

These Eyes

Sever this kiss from me,

And take it with you

While you are at it,

Take these solemn eyes as well;

For they are only worthwhile having in your presence

Without you, there is no light

All that I am is perception

The perception of you

Without you, I am an empty observer

Uninterested in anything else

If I had your Kiss

Slowly I close my eyes

Tears cease to exist

I understand

Life is not perfect by design

You don't need all that I offer

Nor the little I can give

Tonight I believe in God

I understand

This is just one of those things, I guess

I will not beg, nor will I harass

I am no stranger to disappointment

I have seen the fires of hell before

They do not scare me

I will do my best not to stare

I will do what I can, not to care

Because I understand

I accept your decision cold

— Bitter taste on my lips

But I truly do care

So I will not add to the turmoil, to your distress

I will bow out gracefully, with my honor partly intact

I will give you peace of mind

I will respect all of your decisions

I understand — nothing

This cold numbing feeling grows deep in my heart

As my hopes are slowly kissed and laid to rest;

Like a mother to a child ...I will remember the dance

I will not forget the dreams

And I will always wonder

What nights would be like, if I had your kiss

Walls

Tonight I stare gently at the waves

They ebb back and forth echoing the sighs in my heart

I have come to terms with defeat

-- You don't want me. I can't say I blame you,

For what in God's name could I do for you anyway?

I hear the Siren's song

It's calling, beckoning for me to enter her waves

Calling me to enter the long slumber cold

But I have been through this before

and there is no promise in that

Droplets of water caress my face

For the moment I picture your hands

Touching my face, healing my heart

My God, will I leave this place devoid of true love?

Never knowing what it would be like to kiss you?

To hold you in the rain?

To feel your hands on my face?

There is a great sadness here

I believe I have put the world to shame tonight

I don't see the justice of it all

Perhaps I deserve this somehow, although I doubt it

For all my deeds, good and evil, have been justified

The waves ebb back and forth

They reflect life, death and life once again

Tonight I call forth the Siren and I dare her to join me

Tonight I beckon her to my deep waters

So that I may be touched once again

My standards are high, Sometimes too high for most

I have spent too many years building walls

and destroying hopes

Downward Spirals

Once again I am at the water's edge

This time I accept it all

I sense the boundaries ever strong

The barrier came down hard between us tonight

If my heart had a skull,

it would be crushed by now

If my soul had skin,

it would glimmer with indigo bruises

I surrender myself again to the waters of your sea

But there is no hope

I am the hue in motion

Gliding ever downward,

Nothing can save me now

Your eyes now see through me,

As though I no longer exist

Therefore, I do not

Your smile hits hard

It is an anchor you willingly give to me

to help my descent

Life flows through me,

I am in constant motion

Downward spirals, but in motion nonetheless

Fires rage deep inside,

My laughter, mad and intoxicated

I raise my arms daring for more and more and more

The fires rage deep below the sea

I am on the verge of numbness

Nothing can save me now – Nothing!

The fires still rage and all I can manage to do is laugh

I have finally gone mad. This is life and there is no salvation

The madness consumes me -- The fire below your sea

The fires calm, but all is not perfect

Yet they settle into perfect harmony

Embers of madness are all that remain of me now

Do you remember me? The kiss?

The gentle smoke in our thoughts?

Will you remember or will you regret?

Now everything I am or was is like a strange shadow on the moon

It's there - hidden and waiting

It is yours if you put the effort to search for it

But I am afraid that it will be barely worth the trouble when you find it

The fire goes to sleep deep below your sea

Shhh, quietly, no one to notice the last flicker

No one to sing a last lullaby

The beautiful becomes the beautiful

Shhh, it is okay you did nothing wrong

Creole Charm

Vile, wanting; you send for me

Wicked words and dirty hands

Lustful heat and dilated eyes

You summon me

Fiery black dream your hands demand

I refuse with every part of me

But you hold the words,

The Creole charm over me

The wicked words your mother taught you

The same words she used on me

Glittering scars, sweet reminders of your mother's lust

Streak my broken back like stars across black sky

Like always I cave, my throat thirsts for you

I'm here now, do what you will ... Make me hate you

Palero's Night

Fresh rain on the ground stares at a lost soul

It reminds me of the dream I once had

On a slow barge, on a warm moonlit night

A powerful Palero's night, mystical like purple hue

Magic and ether hang heavy in the air

It is a night of in between worlds

The lone boatman, whom I can't see,

Navigates a rickety old barge with a single pole

Majestic slow strokes, like dreams upon smoke

All around me headstones, and crosses

Forgotten temples for the dead

A cemetery submerged under water -- waist deep

Wild vines everywhere and the vivid sense

of being watched

Heaven and the Ether, they watch

Drums, deep inside my chest, rumble silently

yielding no sound only emotion

Yellow eyes glowing, rolling to the back of his head,

his gapping crooked smile lets me know

that he is in-between places

One foot here and one foot somewhere else

He says to me: "Beware of the Mad Unicorn,

for it is a tragic thing gone wrong"

The words move up and down my back like

a lover's heated caress

Fear races like wicked tongues of flames

skipping across my neck and down my back

I can feel the creature staring at me

I think I see him -- I am afraid to look

The rain on the ground stares at a lost scared soul

My eyes open, and the words echo

"Beware of the Mad Unicorn, for it is a tragic thing

gone wrong"

I look up and about me trying to get a bearing,

Trying to feel something

But I realize the dark truth, for this storm is not over

This calm is just the eye of the storm

I look up through this portal to the heavens

and I see the stars

The moon and the angels all in awe or in shock

They stare down at me each helpless to do anything, agony clear in their

eyes

Something has gone wrong in creation

and we all know it

The calm is temporary

for eye of the storm is on the move

I dread this place in the cold dark of the storm

I knew that your waters were deep and I knew that

your waters were cold

But I had no idea that it would be so dark down here

-- At the bottom of your sea

Inner peace is gone and the lights begin to fade

-- The angels bow their heads in shame

It is not bad enough that you have become consuming

Like ubiquitous dark sea

No, now you must also become the storm in my sky

The blackness comes and I have no strength to muster

I close my eyes and I hear the swelling of your sea

Your scent heavy in the wind

It is all over ... A Unicorn is laughing,

Somewhere in the dark of your bitter sea

A Breath Away

I no longer speak of love

The thought of the flawed concept burns

It burns and sanitizes all that I am

Why give me heart if I cannot be with you?

A love with you

A love clean

Free of Sin

Free of Distortion

Free of Judgment, Free

A love like that is always out of reach

A love like that is always for someone else

A love where I can rest my head

Close my eyes

Know that all is well... A love like that is always a breath away

At the Foot of my Bed

Softly, gently, you crept into my bedroom

Gliding on rose petals guided by tears

You sat at the foot of my bed

Once again, at the foot of my bed

My eyes sensed you before I sensed you

So I awoke to find you there, at the foot of my bed

I sat up, tears swelling waiting for a cue

You no longer hover over me,

Not even in my dreams anymore

You just sit there and stare at me

The sigh in your heart is hidden from me now

Yet it deafens me to no end

Your eyes tell of oh so many things,

You are the Siren that answered the call

But you have nothing to say to me

I guess, sometimes there is nothing to say

I can't change anything at all

Not who I am, and definitely not you

If I could I would surrender all that I have

But all I have are sighs, at the foot of my bed

When the Stars Give Way

Will love ever be just?

Will it ever play fair and be noble like

the balance between Earth and Sea?

Will it ever give up its predatory nature?

When will love be like a soothing body of warm water?

Love will be love until the stars give way

Stand

I embrace the storm to come

My chest is empty and hollow like a poor man's kettle

I have no tears left because I am done with it

Done with this thing I have clung to all my life

Love is the constant division between Heaven and Earth

Tonight my veils giveaway, Eyes closed

Heart and soul bound by faith

With arms wide open I welcome your sting

I welcome the cold of your steel

I know no fear anymore

All that could be taken, Has been taken

Let me love eternal, Let me love true No matter what the price

For I rather perish knowing that I took a stand

Then to live a life sheltered and little

King

I am King

And you, you are my crown

I am the Papa King

King of the dinosaurs

King of the Elephants

King of the Pumpkin patch

And you, you are my Pumpkin

You are my crown

When I get too serious, you lean forward

tilting off the side of my head,

Reminding me of who I am

Silly like you

A kid just like you

You are my crown

You are my joy

Stay little

Stay with me

I hope not to let you down

But sometimes even kings are not perfect

One day you will be Queen

Queen of the dinosaurs

Queen of the Elephants

Queen of your own Pumpkin patch

You will have your own Crown

and your own Pumpkins

I hope I get to see your crown,

and your pumpkins

You are the best part of me

You are the best part of Mother Mermaid

Don't forget me

Stay little

Stay with me

Even though new tides may guide you away

to a new land

To new home

Don't forget me

Stay little

Stay with me

I am king only because you are my crown

Every Dream Shattered

Rain bear down on me with Heaven's full weight

Each raindrop is a reminder of every heart I have broken and every dream that has shattered

The shimmer and gloss on the ground is a lonesome reflection of disappointment

Drudging forward to the drum like murmuring echoes of collapsing hopes

Cold wind and dead leaves are all that are left of a life wasted in vice

But then I think of you and know that there is something more

Something greater than myself or my misadventures

How horrible could I have possibly been if you are still with me?

You are the beautiful flaw in this masterpiece of misery and ruin

You are the proverbial silver lining to my cloudy day

If true love is a journey then surely you must be the compass by which such beauty guides itself

Dare my Heart Ponder?

Dare my heart ponder? Love?

It is so difficult to sound genuine with this cold medium

Life, my cold medium

Know this, if anything ever, know this - I am moved by you

Like frothy sea by sudden gale

I am moved by the possibilities you summon within me

Once again, the illusion of hope seduces me

The promise of promise smiles upon me

It offers a gentle hand

It is the gravity that promises to gently pull me in

I believe in you

I believe in what we could be - I believe in fire

The fire I feel for you - The fire I feel when I am with you

Only with you ... One foot off the ledge ... Leap with me?

Show Me This

Show me fire like Supernovas running wild

Show me stars not afraid to crash and burn

Give me what I see in You

Give me what I can sense in us

Give me Love

Magnificent, End of the World, love

That In-between Place

I woke up feeling lost and somewhat still in a daze

My Soul still firmly rooted in that beautiful place

That in-between place

The scent of your mouth still lingering on my fingers

You have changed me

Things have changed

The world is no longer the same

Put your hands on my face

Tell me that you are as real as the rain

And I will believe you

Noise

The actions of others make noise

Irritating and malevolent noise

The black noise

The noise of insanity

Echoes of the insane

Like jet engine turbines growling at my ears

Screaming, screeching; bleeding my ears

Tearing at my soul

Bleeding me

The emerging clamor engulfs me

in a whirlwind of stupidity

It smothers life from me

Black din to strangle me beneath its heaviness

The din turning my sanity into insanity

Vulgar rant, green and ill with vile   intent,

Drowns the good in me

The noise suffocates me

I see no end

I see no end until I see you

You blanket me in pause

Your name is fortitude and serenity

Your name, is a good word

A word to calm the storm

To hush the din

Your name is a sweet melody,

Like a lullaby

Your name soothes me

You are here, now all goes quiet

With you by my side, I can dream again

Roar

My thoughts are with you and know

in your heart that I am with you true

Somewhere between the Fog and the Doubt

Beneath the veil of darkness,

like a glimmer of hope

Hope with a beautiful voice

Not a whisper, not a murmur, but a roar

A Roaring Thunder of promise

Like a million Silver-Hoofed Stallions

Galloping across the Gold laden streets

of an ancient city

Words

Trivial secondhand words will never do

Never for someone like you

Fiery lover of warm skin and somber eyes

Failed Paradigms and Archetypes do no justice

Only the sincere reserve of words will do

No soul has ever felt what I feel for you

No saint has ever known passion the likes

you ignite within me

No catastrophic lover has kissed as sweetly

as I have with you

I alone hold the key to an ocean

A reserve of words fathoms deep, as it is wide

I hold the key in my ardent words when I draw

near your soul

It is in my mouth when I glide over   the subtle straits of your neck

It is in my words when I speak of you to the heavens

The key, I hold in my hand when I hold your hand and caress your skin

Trivial secondhand words will never do

Never in a million years for someone like you

You summon words unknown to me

Speaking in tongues, the new language of love,

True Love

Words that can only exist in a place like Heaven

From Heaven, to my heart,

From my heart to my lips

From my lips to your ears

In heaven there is a blissful ocean of words

Just for you and I

If the Sea were to Sway

Gently, I move along, whirling, smiling

In my head, a subtle song

My feet barely touch the ground

I'm not part of this place anymore

How I remember those sad days of constant heartbreak

Days desolate black and long before you

Now seem like a lifetime away

If the stars were to no longer shine

I know you would share that with me

If the Sea were to sway, I know you would want me there with you as well

It is as though everything has led me to you

And every price paid was well worth the suffering

Brittle Sea of Misplaced Souls

There is the word

The word is love

The word is hope

The word is both

The word is a path that leads to a sacred place

A place of sheltering fog and subtle light

Me? I was lost

Lost in a brittle sea of misplaced souls

Held down my by a thousand anchors

Always holding on to fruitless intentions

Somewhere in this brittle sea of misplaced souls,

there is you and your eyes

Your eyes show me who I truly am

There is nothing your eyes could not forgive

I'll do all I can to keep you from   turning away

Nothing I wouldn't do to keep you smiling

With your kiss I can deflect a thousand arrows

I see you, only you and your mouth

With your mouth, I find my true voice

Your mouth delivers me

Your mouth is salvation

Your mouth drives me

Your mouth is the switch

I let go and something ravenous now takes over

Your lips beckon me

I thrust forward

Lips upon lips, Tongues entwined

There is no escape, There is no tomorrow

There is just you and I

In this Brittle Sea of misplaced souls

Beauty and Strength

I stare at you and I am mesmerized

As though I have discovered something new

Something pure, something luscious

To think that I was afraid of what was to come

Now I let your eyes ignite the path to a good place

I thought I knew beauty, Now I know beauty

I thought I knew strength, Now I know real strength

Your blue eyes reign over my dominion

Like the celestial grace of an age long past

Like the sky over a humbled and battered land

Like an ocean above my watery grave

Like truth in a whirlwind of lies, Like beauty in the fog of corrosion

Like you my love, like you

My Beloved

Fear not

Doubt not

Worry not

For you are Red Wine and Cheesecake

beneath an autumn night

Even if this tide should turn

I will be with you

Listen to the timbre of the silence between us

It is not a feigning wail dusted in sorrow

But rather a slow deep breath drawn

before our next leap

Fear not

Doubt not

Worry not

For you are Vegas and all her   Glory

beneath an Ocean of Stars

I am with you, no matter what

I am with you

Indigo Girl

You, now so out of place

Lost, you, look to the winds

Find your bearings

Find you courage

Where have you gone?

This life now is cold and so uninvolved

Find your faith, find yourself

Come home, come find me

Sad little girl with Indigo eyes

Come home

Come home

If I could take it all back, I would

This place holds little magic without you

Come take my hand inhale deep and invigorating

Count backwards lets reset this   accident

I can feel the Autumn air on our skin

I can almost taste your kiss

I can feel your smile upon me

Three Two one...

The Hue and The Ghost

I am not the product of fanfare

Nor am I the result of love

I am a coincidence

Fragile and singular

I stand alone, even when I feel the touch of another

I am alone

My barriers are great and vast

My shelter becomes my shell

In turn, my shell becomes my prison

I am alone

It takes a lot to get to me

Even more to get through to me

There is an ether of solitude

It binds and separates me from Heaven, and Earth,

and all theaters in between

I have seen and felt with great impunity

Still I have little in the way of recall

And it takes so much out of me to know,

That ... All that is; is exactly just that

Nothing more and nothing less

Nothing sacred

I wait and wait for salvation

But I fear that it will probably pass me by or

forget my face

I wait for grace to return, so that I may be seen again

Seen not for my fading presence,

but for inner strength and courage

Let grace open your eyes so that you may see the real me; and feel my

roar like that of a fiery green eyed

lion adorned in golden robes

Let majestic strength, which I know and recognize deep within me, make it self open to you

Like you, my love, I am more than this mere frail shadow

I am the hue and the ghost, not just the emotive shell

I know that somewhere inside I am beautiful and

even though my shell gives little or no hint of it, I am

It does take faith

It takes the newfound faith of the faithless

As they come face to face with oblivion to see the hue

To touch the ghost

You and I are not too different - You and I are not too alike

I offer you no hope -- for I have no hope to offer

I only offer you strong arms to hold you down when

Your storm hits I offer you eyes, deep and dark, to guide you through

the tempest in your heart

Let us hold hands -- For the night is long

The Good Rain

Eyes forward little girl

The good rain comes

I love you, I miss you

Even though sometimes I feel that you're not with me

Even though I fear that your heart wanders

Even though I can see the echo of kisses meant for someone else still in

your eyes

Even though I can taste the bitterness of your broken heart on your lips

I cannot undo what has been done to you

Either you are with me or you are not

Come what May, Come what May

I hold no fear in my heart

Because there is no room for it

I am fearless

I am invincible

Do your lips miss me? Me?

My lips miss you

... Only You

Fireflies

Where have you gone?

To that place where the fireflies wont find you?

Let your dreams blue guide your way

Can you hear my gentle song in the wind?

Let it find you and guide you back to my arms

My ocean is empty without you

November Dawn

Wish I could breathe you in

Hold you in my chest, close to my heart

Beneath a winter sky

Like Monarchs in November dawn

Color wings against cold gentle breeze

Gold upon gold, Rare ...On the verge of demise

Beautiful butterfly at the wrong time

But no time can be wrong by your side

Tragic... Limited dream with unlimited thirst to quench

Your kiss will echo long after you are gone

We Glide over Stars

Walk with me

Like me

Barefoot through this valley of vipers

Let them hiss vile and covetous

Let them rattle impotent cries

You are with me so I know no fear

Kisses like the living

Romance like the dead

Purple flowers instead of red

Vipers amongst vipers

We are who we are

Which is why they tread sour ground

and we glide over stars...

A Prayer of Gratitude

Never forget that once upon a time

there was nothing but sorrow

Never forget ; that once cold nights

seemed without end

Never forget the thousand souls that stood in our way

Never forget the Void that once loomed heavy over all horizons

Never forget that things were not always this good

Never forget and rejoice

For it is with a clean heart that we remember

And it is with a clean heart that we are grateful

About the Author …

Gustavo Lapis Ahumada

I am a Romantic and I am a Poet. I believe in loving deeply even when knowing that the outcome will be disastrous. It's what I do, it is simply who I am. My poetry, very much like my music, is forged in the torrent of misadventure and heartache. My words have been described as though Rumi and Neruda were trading war stories by a lonesome fire.

I was born in Argentina and came here to New York City at the young age of six. Son of a world class boxer who made his fortune in the boxing ring, I know a thing or two about fighting battles. Boxing and Love have more in common than most people realize. Both require sense of strategy, strength, the ability to take a hit and most of all a pure heart.

I am a singer/song writer for NYC's own "Bitter Grace"; a fiery Goth Rock band known for its mesmerizing lyrics and heavy club influenced grooves. My music has always has been a deep, dark descent into madness.

As of most recent I am at the helm of a new musical project called "Crimson Brulée". As always, the music reflects the battered soul of its maker with equal amounts of hurt and rage; and the right amount echoing passion. My heart wrenching words will inevitably lead you back to that place which we all have come to fear.

For more information on Gustavo and his music please look for his musical projects (Bitter Grace, Crimson Brulee' and The Witch-Kings) on iTunes, Spotify and all other digital platforms.

Made in the USA
Columbia, SC
18 February 2021